What Are Citizens' Basic Rights?

By William David Thomas

Gareth Stevens
Publishing

Please visit our web site at www.garethstevens.com. For a free catalog describing Gareth Stevens Publishing's list of high-quality books, call 1-800-542-2595 (USA) or 1-800-387-3178 (Canada). Gareth Stevens Publishing's fax: 1-877-542-2596

Library of Congress Cataloging-in-Publication Data

Thomas, William, 1947–
    What are citizens' basic rights? / William David Thomas.
        p. cm.—(My American government)
    Includes bibliographical references and index.
    ISBN-10: 0-8368-8861-8   ISBN-13: 978-0-8368-8861-4 (lib. bdg.)
    ISBN-10: 0-8368-8866-9   ISBN-13: 978-0-8368-8866-9 (softcover)
    1. Civil rights—United States—Juvenile literature.   I. Title.
    KF4749.T46   2007
    342.7308'5—dc22   2007032425

This edition first published in 2008 by
Gareth Stevens Publishing
A Weekly Reader® Company
1 Reader's Digest Road
Pleasantville, NY 10570-7000 USA

Copyright © 2008 by Gareth Stevens, Inc.

Senior Managing Editor: Lisa M. Guidone
Creative Director: Lisa Donovan
Cover Designer: Jeannie Friedman
Interior Designer: Yin Ling Wong
Photo Researchers: Kimberly Babbitt and Charlene Pinckney

Picture credits: Cover, title page: Win McNamee/Getty Images; p. 5 © Keith Brofsky/Maxx Images; p. 7 The Granger Collection; p. 8 The Granger Collection; p. 9 Kevork Djansezian/AP; p. 11 © Bettmann/Corbis; p. 14 Roger Mahony/Getty Images; p. 16 Dwaine Scott/AP/NBC Newswire; p. 17 © Saed Hindash/Star Ledger/Corbis; p. 18 © Bettmann/Corbis; p. 21 Comstock/Corbis; p. 22 Bill Fritsch/Maxx Images; p. 23 © Kim Kulish/Corbis; p. 24 © David Butlow/Corbis; p. 28 © Peter Turnley/Corbis; p. 29 © John Neubauer/Photo Edit

Printed in the United States of America

1 2 3 4 5 6 7 8 9 10 09 08 07

Contents

Words in the glossary appear in **bold** type
the first time they are used in the text.

CHAPTER 1

★

Brains and Brawn

Seth was excited. Every September, soon after school began, the four elementary schools in his town had a contest. Eight students were chosen from each school. Each student had to compete in one sports activity and one school subject. The teachers called it the Academic-Athletic Challenge. The kids called it the "Brains and Brawn Battle."

Team members were chosen by the kids at each school. Voting was today. Many kids had made posters about themselves or their friends. They were hanging in the halls.

Seth's specialties were math and football. He enjoyed math. And he could throw a football farther than anyone at his school. Seth knew he would make the team. He was pretty sure his buddy Tony would, too. Tony was a whiz at science and rarely missed a free throw in basketball. Then there was Jennifer. She ran the fifty-yard dash and was really fast. And she was the school spelling champion. But who else would be on the team?

When Seth got to school that morning, he looked for the ballot boxes for voting. They should have been on a table by the school office, but they weren't there. As he walked down the hall, he saw that all of the posters were gone.

All U.S. citizens have **rights**. Rights are freedoms that the government protects. As citizens, young people should know their rights.

Seth hurried to his classroom. Mr. Mancuso wasn't there. A new teacher pointed at him and said, "You! Bring that backpack to me!" Seth handed it over. The teacher looked through it and pulled out a book about Seth's favorite football team.

The teacher scowled at him and said, "I'm keeping this. And you are in big trouble, young man."

Seth stared at him in disbelief. Something was wrong in his school. Something was very wrong.

CHAPTER 2

★

The Bill of Rights

Seth didn't know what to do. The new teacher had taken his book and still had his backpack.

"Where is your seat?" the teacher demanded.

"I sit by the window," Seth answered.

"Well, not any more," said the teacher. He pointed to two high school students near the door. "They will be sitting at that table. You can stand or sit on the floor."

Seth was so shocked he was speechless. He thought, "This can't be happening in my school. Can it?"

The Revolutionary War

What happened to Seth in school that day happened to many Americans long ago. It wasn't their backpacks that were searched. Their homes and businesses were searched without permission. They didn't lose their seats to other students. They were forced to let foreign soldiers live in their homes. The **Revolutionary War** (1775–1783) was fought to gain freedom from England. After the war, Americans formed their own government.

A New Government

The first plan for America's government was called the Articles of Confederation. But the Articles created a weak government that had almost no power. In the summer of 1787, a group of men met in Philadelphia. They came up with a new plan for a government. This plan was the **U.S. Constitution**. By 1789, all of the states had **ratified**, or approved, the Constitution. This created the government we still have today.

The Constitution described the powers of the states and the powers of the U.S. government. It did not describe the rights of the people. Many Americans worried about that. They were afraid that if their rights were not written down, they might be taken away. In fact, some states ratified the Constitution only because James Madison of Virginia promised to add a list of rights to it.

This painting shows the signing of the U.S. Constitution in Philadelphia, Pennsylvania. The famous document was signed on September 17, 1787.

The First Ten Amendments

James Madison is often called the "Father of the Constitution" because he helped write the famous document. He and the other **framers** knew that the country would grow and change. They knew that the Constitution would have to grow and change, too. Madison wanted the first **amendments**, or changes, to the Constitution to be a list of the people's rights.

The Bill of Rights lists the ten amendments that protect the freedoms of people in the United States.

Madison wrote seventeen amendments. They listed and protected people's rights. Congress approved twelve of the amendments. These were sent to the states for approval. By 1791, the states had ratified ten of the amendments. They became part of the U.S. Constitution. These ten amendments are called the **Bill of Rights**.

- The **First Amendment** protects freedom of religion, speech, and the press. This amendment gives people the right to hold peaceful meetings and marches. It also gives people the right to ask the government to change laws they consider unfair.
- The **Second Amendment** gives Americans the right to own firearms.

Thousands of people gathered in Los Angeles in May 2006 to demand rights for **immigrants**. The First Amendment guarantees people the right to hold peaceful demonstrations.

- The **Third Amendment** guarantees that people don't have to let soldiers live in their homes.
- The **Fourth Amendment** protects people from unreasonable searches and seizures. The government cannot take people's property or search their homes or businesses unless they have a good reason.

TO KEEP AND BEAR ARMS

The Second Amendment says, *A well regulated Militia, being necessary to the security of a free State, the right of the people to keep and bear Arms, shall not be infringed.* Some people say this means only the army and police should have guns. Others say it means any citizen.

BILL OF RIGHTS DAY

The Bill of Rights was ratified on December 15, 1791. One hundred fifty years later, in 1941, President Franklin D. Roosevelt declared December 15 to be "Bill of Rights Day." The president urged Americans to fly the flag that day. It was a good time to raise the flag and think about the country's freedoms. Just eight days before, on December 7, Japan had attacked Pearl Harbor in Hawaii. The United States had entered World War II. Today on December 15, civil rights groups hold meetings and events to honor the Bill of Rights. In many schools, students are asked to read and talk about those rights.

- The **Fifth, Sixth,** and **Seventh Amendments** protect the rights of citizens in court. They say that people who are arrested have the right to a fair trial. They give people the right to trial by a **jury**, the right to a lawyer, the right to be told why they have been **accused** of a crime, and the right to have witnesses who will tell their side of the story.
- The **Eighth Amendment** protects citizens from cruel or unusual punishment.
- The **Ninth Amendment** covers rights besides those in the Constitution. It was James Madison's way of saying, "Just because we forgot to list a right doesn't mean Americans don't have that right!"

- The **Tenth Amendment** protects the powers of the states. It says states can make their own laws as long as they agree with the Constitution.

These amendments were the first additions to the Constitution. But they were not the last.

More Amendments

More than 11,000 amendments have been proposed since the Constitution was written. But only seventeen have been added since the first ten amendments. In 1865, the Thirteenth Amendment made slavery illegal in the United States. In 1870, the Fifteenth Amendment guaranteed that a person could not be denied the right to vote because of race or color. In 1920, the Nineteenth Amendment gave women the right to vote. The newest amendment, the Twenty-Seventh, was added in 1992.

The Fifteenth Amendment gave African American men the right to vote. This drawing shows former slaves voting for the first time.

CHAPTER 3

★

First Amendment Freedoms

The new teacher called the class to order. "I'm Mr. Quirt," he said. "My helpers are Miss Li and Mr. Stein. We're in for Mr. Mancuso today."

"What happened to our posters?" asked Sean.

Mr. Quirt replied, "We took them down. Your opinions don't matter."

Theresa raised her hand. "The school newspaper said that…"

"The school newspaper will no longer be printed," said Mr. Quirt.

"Wait," said Kelly. "We were supposed to have a class meeting this morning to talk about…"

"No meetings!" You don't need to talk about anything. We make the decisions here."

Seth couldn't stand it anymore. "That's not fair!" he shouted.

"Well then," said Mr. Quirt in a nasty voice, "why don't you write a letter to the school board?"

"I will!"

"That's enough!" shouted Mr. Quirt. He turned to Mr. Stein. "Take this boy to the principal's office."

The First Amendment

Mr. Quirt took away several important freedoms. Each of them is guaranteed by the First Amendment to the Constitution. The actual 45 words of the amendment are:

> *"Congress shall make no law respecting an establishment of religion, or prohibiting the free exercise thereof; or abridging the freedom of speech, or of the press; or the right of the people peaceably to assemble, and to petition the Government for a redress of grievances."*

Many people consider the First Amendment the most important one. The writers of the Constitution believed that freedom of religion, speech, and press were important to protect their rights. They also thought that citizens should be able to gather in groups and ask the government to make changes.

KNOW YOUR FREEDOMS

Do you know what freedoms are protected by the First Amendment? Most Americans don't. In 2006, a survey found that many Americans could name three judges on the TV show *American Idol*. Few could name any three freedoms in the First Amendment. The same survey found that many Americans could name all five members of the Simpsons cartoon family. Hardly any could name all five First Amendment freedoms.

Leaders from many different faiths gathered at a ceremony in California. The First Amendment promises religious freedoms that are not allowed in many other countries.

Freedom of Religion

One reason that English settlers first came to America was for religious freedom. Some settlers, however, wanted more than that. A group called the Puritans came to Massachusetts. They wanted to be free from the rules of English churches. The First Amendment says people can practice any religion they chose, or none at all. It also says the government cannot force people to follow a certain religion. There can't be an "official" religion in America.

Freedom of Speech

According to the First Amendment, Americans have the right to speak their opinions on any subject. That includes talking in public, on television or radio, writing letters and newspaper stories, or even making movies. Americans can say almost anything, but they cannot threaten people or their property. And freedom of speech does not give people the right to say or print something harmful about a person when they know those statements aren't true.

THE HIGH COST OF FREE SPEECH

When candidates run for office today, they must buy time on television and radio to explain their ideas. This is very expensive. Every election year, some groups complain. They say that only people with lots of money are able to speak to Americans. This, they say, **violates** the Constitution's rule about free speech. They want to control spending. That way, all candidates would get equal "air time." Other groups say the opposite. They believe that limiting the money candidates can spend limits free speech. What do you think?

With a microphone and high rubber boots, Brian Williams of NBC News reports from New Orleans after Hurricane Katrina in August 2005. Many reporters said the government did a poor job of helping people after the storm. The First Amendment protects freedom of the press, which includes TV news networks.

Freedom of the Press

When the Bill of Rights was written, "the press" meant newspapers and books. Today it also means television, radio, and the Internet. The media must be able to print or broadcast all of the news. In some countries, the press is controlled by the government. There, people read, see, and hear only stories approved by the government. According to the First Amendment, people in the United States have the right to publish and read books, newspapers, and magazines of their choice.

DON'T READ THAT BOOK?

For hundreds of years, groups of people have tried to **ban** books they don't like. They have tried to stop people from selling or reading them. Many other people say Americans should be free to buy and read any books they choose. They believe the First Amendment gives them that right. Every year, the American Library Association has a Banned Book Week. It celebrates freedom of speech and freedom of the press. Maybe you've read some of the banned books listed here.

- All of the Harry Potter books, by J.K. Rowling
- *Blubber*, by Judy Blume
- *Bridge to Terabithia*, by Katherine Paterson
- *James and the Giant Peach*, by Roald Dahl
- *The Witches*, by Roald Dahl

This girl couldn't wait to start reading the seventh and final Harry Potter title, *Harry Potter and the Deathly Hollows*.

In August 1963, more than 200,000 people marched through Washington, D.C. seeking equal rights for African Americans. It was here that Martin Luther King, Jr. made his famous "I Have a Dream" speech.

Freedom of Assembly

The First Amendment protects the right to assemble in groups. This includes political meetings, protest marches, and school board meetings. Americans assemble to welcome home soldiers from overseas. They also assemble to protest against sending soldiers overseas. As long as the events are peaceful, any group can hold a public meeting, march, or demonstration.

Freedom to Petition the Government

Mr. Quirt told Seth to "write a letter to the school board." Seth said he would. That is the right to **petition** the government. It means that citizens can write or talk to people in the government. They can tell officials to do something or to stop doing it. That right is guaranteed by the First Amendment.

CHAPTER 4

★

The Rights of the Accused

Seth was angry. He hadn't done anything wrong. Why had he been sent to the principal? Would the principal call his parents? Then he had an idea. He would call his parents!

Mrs. Rios, the school secretary, was at her desk. She was always kind and helpful. Seth went up to her and said, "Mrs. Rios, may I please use the phone?"

"Another trouble maker, eh?" she snapped. "No, you may not use the phone! You may sit there and be quiet!"

Seth couldn't believe it. "What's going on here?" he wondered.

Due Process of Law

Mr. Quirt acted like Seth was guilty of something. So did Mrs. Rios. But no one told Seth what he had done wrong. There was no one to tell his side of the story. And he wasn't allowed to call for help. The school did not follow "due process of law."

Due process is a set of rules or **procedures**. Many of them are in the Constitution. These procedures are followed each time someone is accused of a crime. This doesn't mean that every person in every case is treated the same. It does mean every person is treated fairly.

Due process begins with a simple but very important idea. You've probably heard of it: a person accused of a crime is innocent until proven guilty. In America, no one has to prove that he or she is innocent. Instead, the government must prove that the person is guilty.

Rights Are Respected

Due process of law means that the rights of an accused person are respected. These rights are spelled out in Amendments Four, Five, and Six of the Constitution.

- Law officers cannot search you, your house, or items that belong to you without "probable cause." That means they must have a very good reason to think that you have committed a crime.
- If you are arrested, you have the right to be told exactly why.
- You have the right to a lawyer to help you. The U.S. Supreme Court has said that if an accused person cannot afford a lawyer, the government must provide one.
- You have the right to a trial before a jury.
- You cannot be made to speak against yourself in court.
- You have the right to see and hear the people who are accusing you.
- You have the right to call on people to tell your side of the story.
- You cannot be tried for the same crime more than once.

These rules have been used by American courts for more than two hundred years. They are only procedures. But as a Supreme Court Justice once said, "The history of American freedom is … the history of procedure."

The Constitution guarantees the right to a trial by a jury. This and other rights ensure that people accused of crimes are treated fairly.

AN OLD IDEA

"No free man shall be arrested, or imprisoned, or deprived of his property ... unless by legal judgment of his peers, or by the law of the land." Those words were written in England eight hundred years ago. They are in a famous document called the *Magna Carta*. The same idea is found in Amendments Six and Seven of the U.S. Constitution.

The Price We Pay

Due process helps to keep innocent people from being wrongfully punished. The system is not perfect, however. Due process sometimes allows a guilty person to go free. But that is the price we pay for a system that protects the rights of all people—even those accused of a crime.

TAKING THE FIFTH

Think about courtroom TV shows or movies you've seen. A character might say, "I refuse to answer on the grounds that I may incriminate myself." Self-incrimination is being forced to say something in court that would make you seem guilty. The Fifth Amendment protects people against this. When people refuse to speak against themselves, it is called, "taking the Fifth."

A lawyer explains the Fifth Amendment rights to his client.

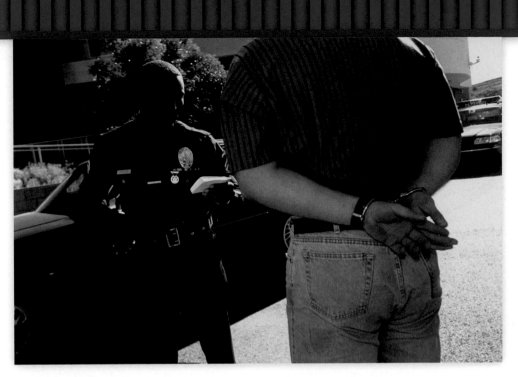

Anyone arrested as a suspect in a crime must be told of his or her rights. This police officer reads the Miranda rights from a note card.

Mr. Miranda's Rights

You've heard it on TV and in movies. When someone is arrested, the police officer makes a short speech. It begins, "You have the right to remain silent…" This is the reason for that speech. In 1963, Arizona police questioned a man about some stolen money. The man, named Miranda, **confessed** to stealing the money. He also confessed to kidnapping a girl. Later, lawyers said Miranda did not know his rights. They said his confession could not be used in court. The case reached the Supreme Court. In 1966, the Supreme Court ruled that police must tell people their rights. Since then, officers must read the "Miranda rights" to anyone they arrest.

★

CHAPTER 5

Citizens' Responsibilities

Mr. Sullivan, the principal, called Seth into his office. "Relax," he said. "You're not in trouble." Now Seth was really confused.

"We put on a little play this morning," Mr. Sullivan explained. "Mr. Quirt, Mrs. Rios, and the others were just acting their parts." Seth started to feel a little better.

"The play was part of a social studies lesson," the principal continued. "This week your class will be learning about the

Schools, court houses, churches—even laundromats—are used as polling places when Americans cast their votes.

rights we enjoy as Americans. Some of your basic rights were taken away this morning. I hope you will remember how it felt. Americans have rights. With those rights come some **responsibilities**. You'll be learning about them, too."

Voting

Americans live in a **democracy**. It is a form of government in which people elect their leaders. The United States has a form of democracy known as a representative democracy. What that means is Americans vote for representatives who speak and act for them in making laws.

One of the most important rights American citizens have is the right to vote. It was one of the reasons Americans fought the Revolutionary War. Colonial laws were made in England. Americans could not vote on those laws or elect the people who made them. They had no representation in the government. Voting makes citizens part of the government.

But voting is more than a right. It is also a duty, or responsibility. It is important for all **eligible** people to vote

FAILING TO VOTE

It seems that many U.S. citizens don't vote. In a recent presidential election, 79 million eligible voters did not vote. People have the right to vote, but many Americans don't use it. Voting gives citizens a voice in their government.

TIME LINE OF VOTING RIGHTS

Women, African Americans, and others struggled for their right to vote. The changes did not come all at once. Groups of people worked hard through the years to help gain their rights. The time line below shows changes in voting rights since the Constitution was ratified.

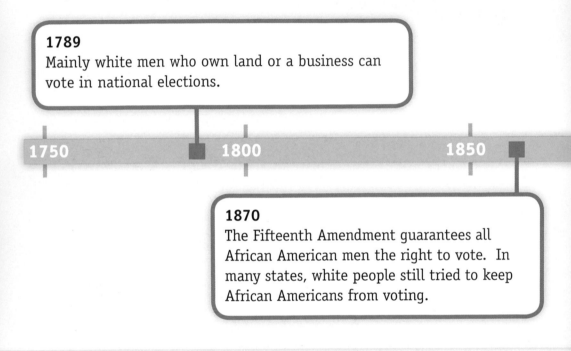

1789
Mainly white men who own land or a business can vote in national elections.

1750   1800   1850

1870
The Fifteenth Amendment guarantees all African American men the right to vote. In many states, white people still tried to keep African Americans from voting.

in every election. Anyone who is eighteen years old, is a citizen of the U.S., and has registered is eligible to vote. People who have the right to vote have the responsibility to be informed voters. They should learn about the candidates and the issues.

Jury Duty

A person accused of a crime has the right to a trial before a jury. With that right comes a responsibility. In most states, a person must be twenty-one years old to be on a jury. Local

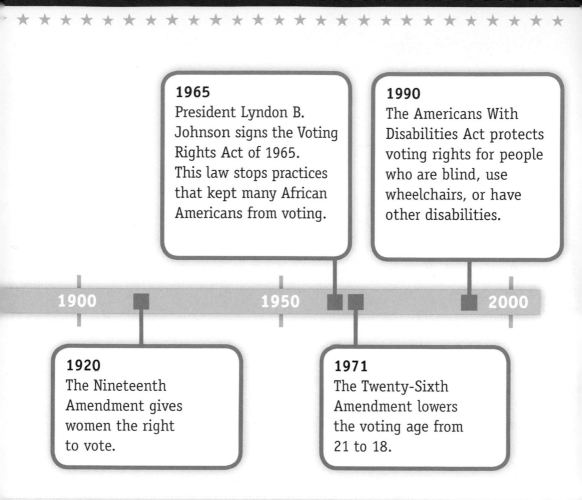

1965
President Lyndon B. Johnson signs the Voting Rights Act of 1965. This law stops practices that kept many African Americans from voting.

1990
The Americans With Disabilities Act protects voting rights for people who are blind, use wheelchairs, or have other disabilities.

1900   1950   2000

1920
The Nineteenth Amendment gives women the right to vote.

1971
The Twenty-Sixth Amendment lowers the voting age from 21 to 18.

governments keep a list of citizens who are eligible for jury duty. People who are chosen have to attend the trial. Most trials are over in a few days, but some may last for months. Jury members must listen carefully to everything that is said. In the end, they must decide if the person on trial is guilty or not.

One of the longest jury trials in U.S. history took place in Illinois. The case was about a train wreck that leaked poison chemicals into a neighborhood. The trial began in 1984 and lasted more than four years.

Military Service

Protecting the country is another responsibility. People are needed in the Army, Navy, Air Force, Marines, and Coast Guard. Men and women may join any branch of the service they choose. Being part of the military is not easy, even in peace time. But serving or being ready to serve is part of the price for keeping our country safe and free.

Today, service in the armed forces is **voluntary**. But many times in U.S. history, during a war, men have been forced to join. This is called a **draft**. If drafted, any man who was healthy enough had to serve. Even today, all men must register for the draft once they are eighteen years old. Under present laws, women do not have to register. They cannot be drafted.

Soldiers of the Georgia National Guard take part in a farewell ceremony before they leave for Iraq.

Jury members listen to a lawyer. Serving on a jury is one of the responsibilities of good citizens.

Responsible Citizens

The Constitution does not list people's responsibilities. It doesn't say they have to vote. It doesn't say they must serve on a jury. But citizens are expected to do these things and more. They are expected to obey the laws of their town, state, and country. They are expected to pay their taxes. These are people's responsibilities as citizens.

People can be responsible citizens in other ways, too. They can take part in town meetings. They can volunteer their time to help local groups. Many citizens, each doing a little, can make a big difference. For example, people can help stop pollution by cleaning up a park near their home. That's part of being a responsible citizen.

Glossary

accuse: to say that a person has done something wrong or illegal

amendment: an official change to the U.S. Constitution

ban: an official order to stop or prevent something

Bill of Rights: the first ten amendments to the U.S. Constitution

confess: saying that you've done something

democracy: a form of government in which people elect their leaders

draft: a system that forces people into military service

eligible: meeting the requirements to do something

framers: the people who wrote the U.S. Constitution

immigrant: a person who leaves his or her home country and comes to a new land to live

jury: a group of people chosen to listen to a case in a court of law and make a decision about the issues involved

petition: a formal request made to a leader or to the government

procedure: a series of steps followed to get something done

ratify: to officially approve something

responsibility: a duty that a person is expected to fulfill

Revolutionary War: the war that the American colonies fought to gain freedom from England (1775–1783)

right: a freedom that is protected by law

U.S. Constitution: the written plan and laws of the U.S. government

violate: failing to obey; to break a rule

voluntary: done of your own free will, without being forced

To Find Out More

Books

The Bill of Rights. We The People (series). Michael Burgan (Compass Point Books)

Constitution Translated for Kids. Cathy Travis (Synergy Books)

Freedom of Assembly. Land of the Free (series). David C. King (Millbrook Press)

Freedom of Speech. True Books (series). Christin Ditchfield (Children's Press)

Web Sites

Ben Franklin's Guide to the U.S. Government
http://bensguide.gpo.gov/6-8/citizenship/index.html

"Concentrating" on the Bill of Rights. Try this card game!
www.quia.com/cc/67829.html

How much do you know about Freedom of Religion? Find out!
www.pbs.org/now/quiz/quiz2.html

The United States Constitution for Kids
www.usconstitution.net/constkids4.html

Publisher's note to educators and parents: Our editors have carefully reviewed these web sites to ensure that they are suitable for children. Many web sites change frequently, however, and we cannot guarantee that a site's future contents will continue to meet our high standards of quality and educational value. Be advised that children should be closely supervised whenever they access the Internet.

Index

About the Author

William David Thomas lives in Rochester, New York, where he works with students who have special needs. Bill claims he was once King of Fiji, but gave up the throne to pursue a career as a relief pitcher. It's not true. He dedicates this book to his children, who always vote (though not always as he does).